DESIGNS FOR RELAXATION AND MINDFUNESS

I ♥ GIRAFFE

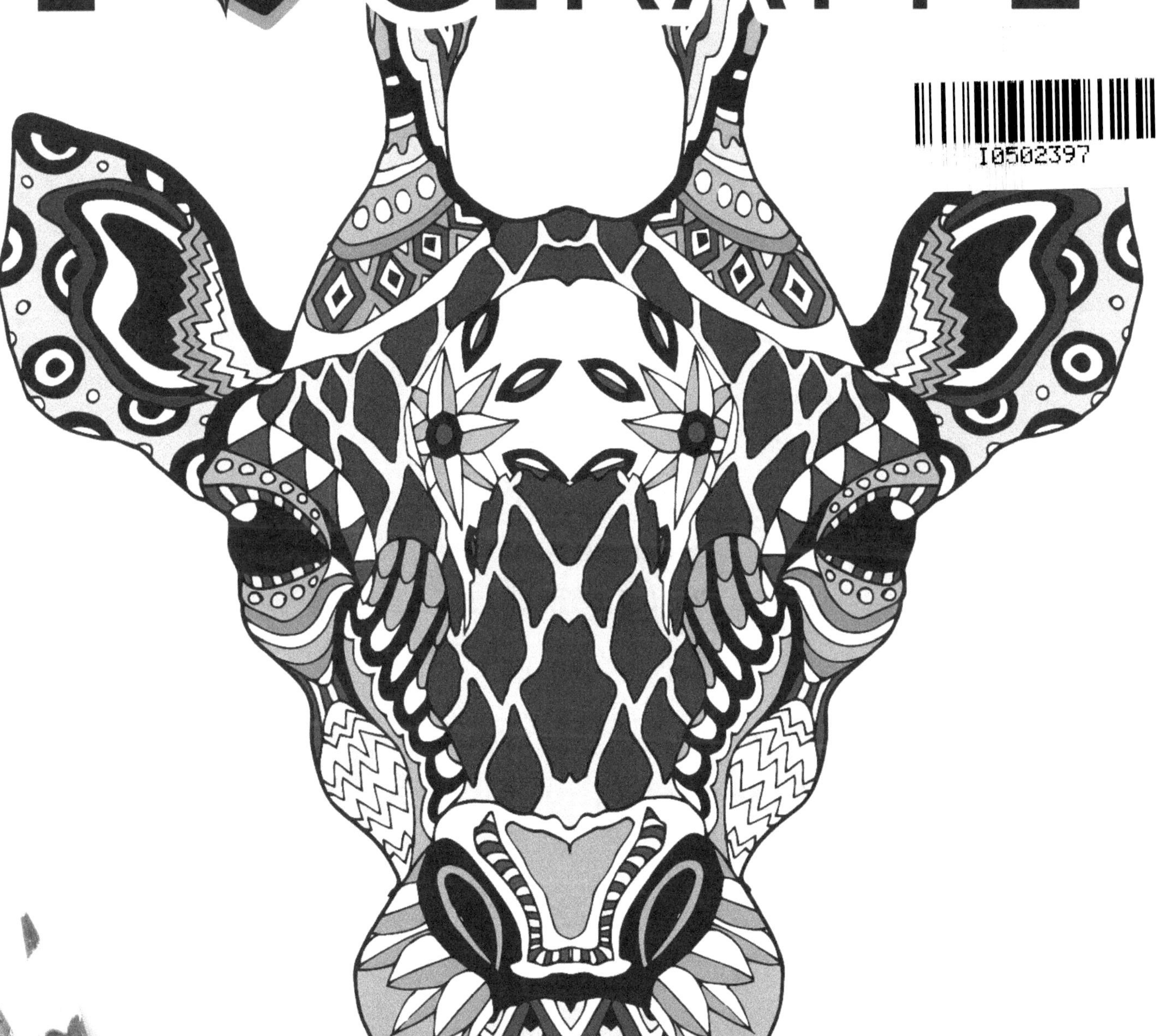

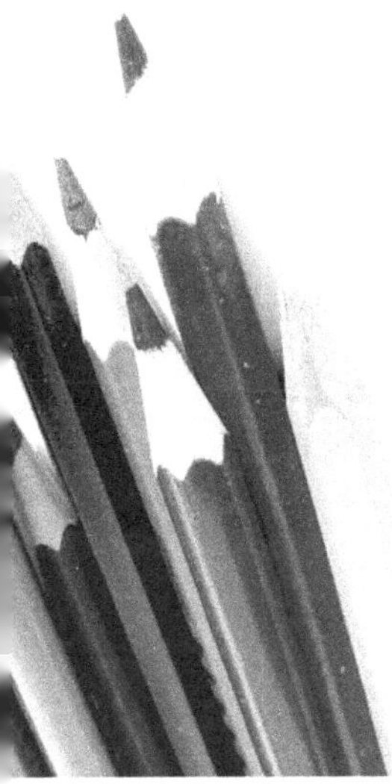

COLORING BOOK FOR ADULTS

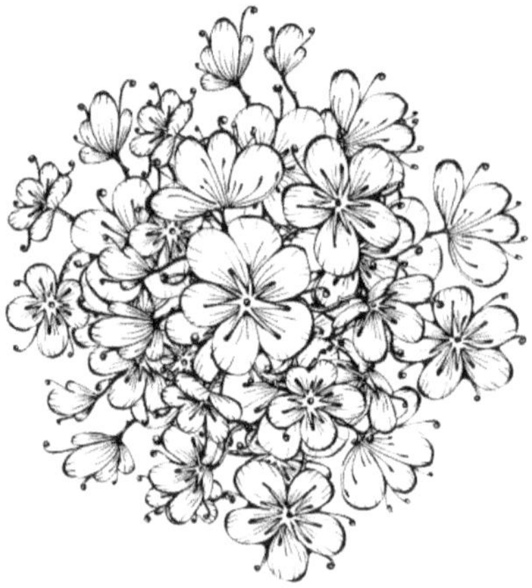

KYOTO SAKURA

Printed in The U.S.A.

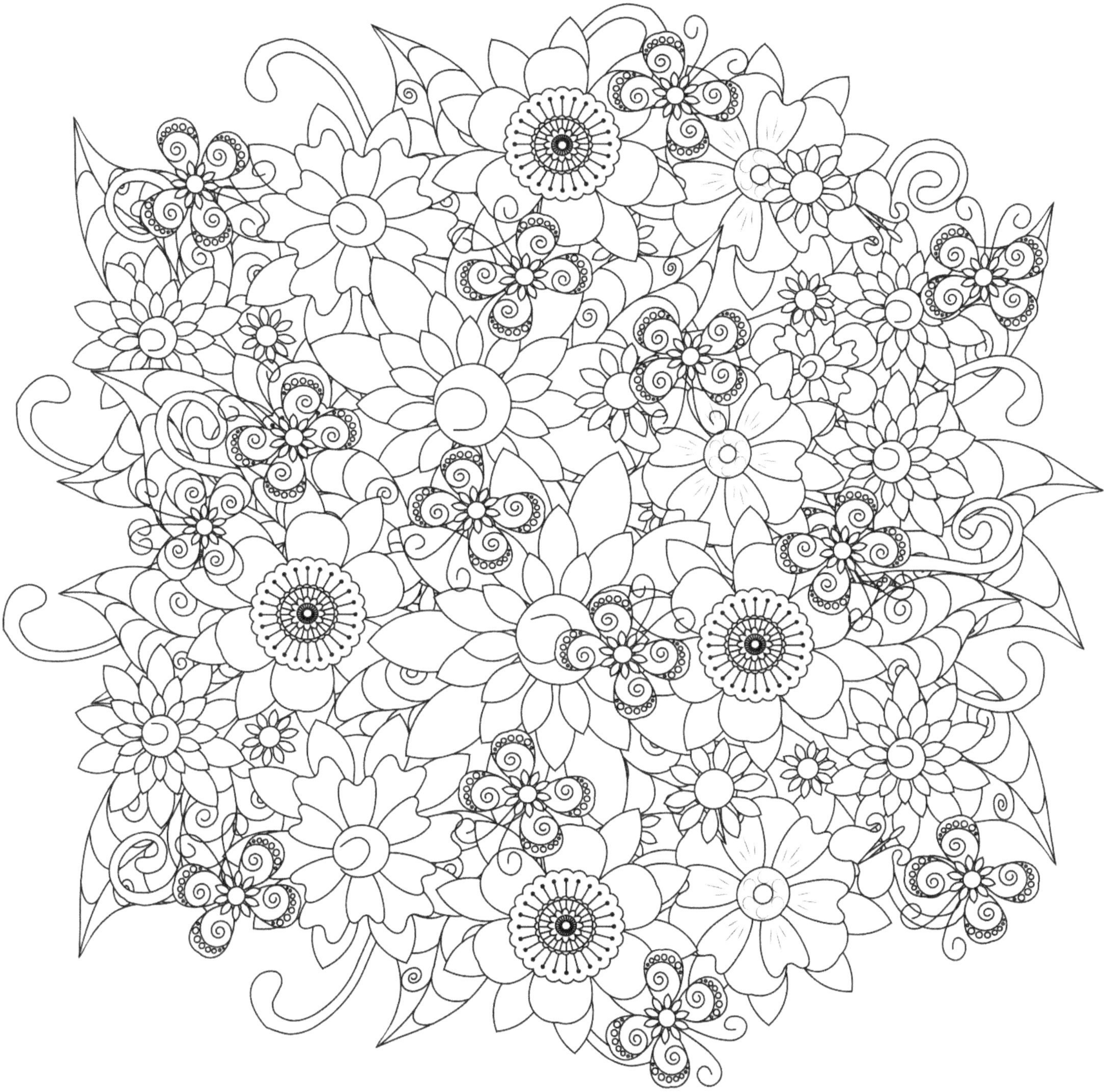

TEST YOUR COLOR

1.

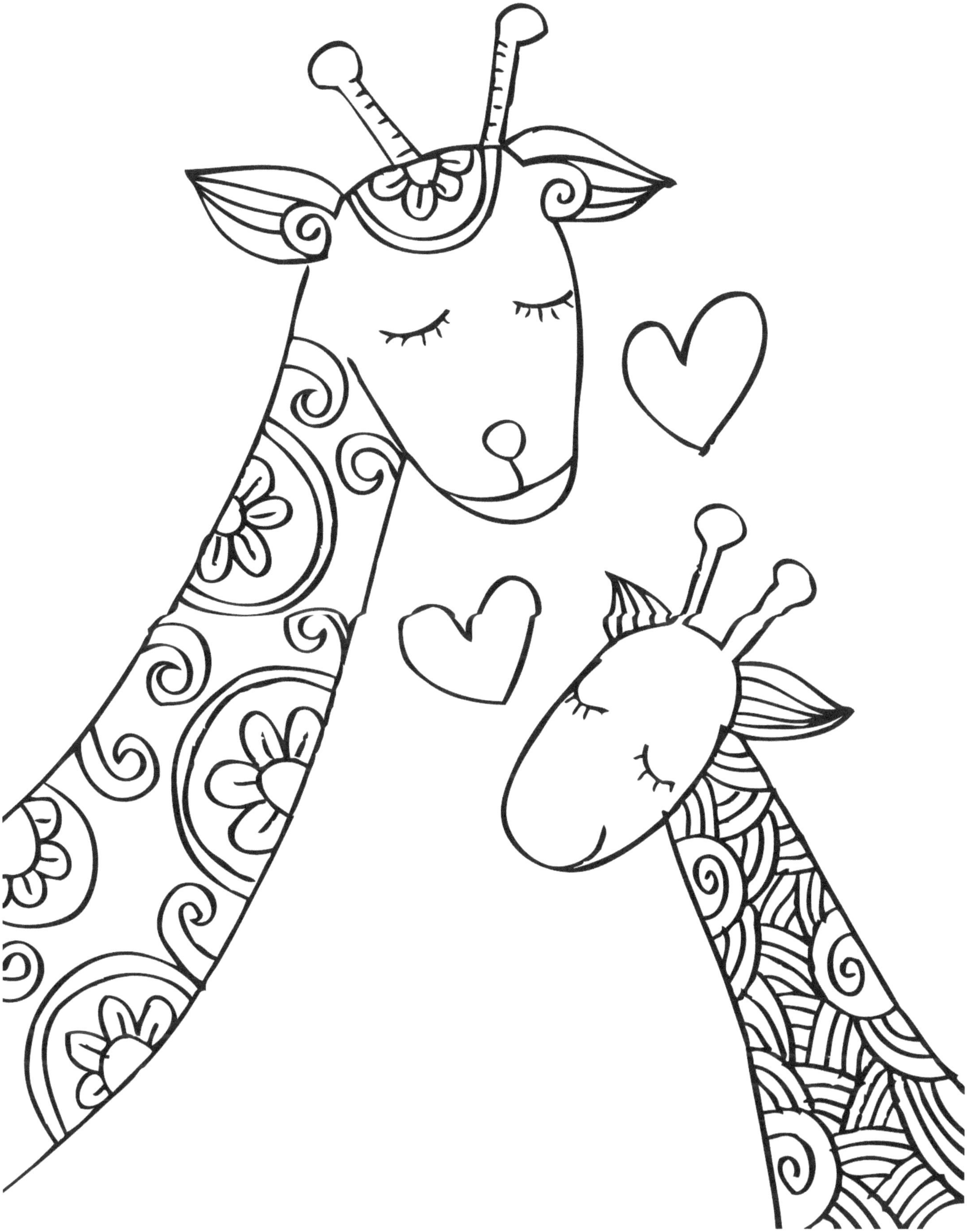

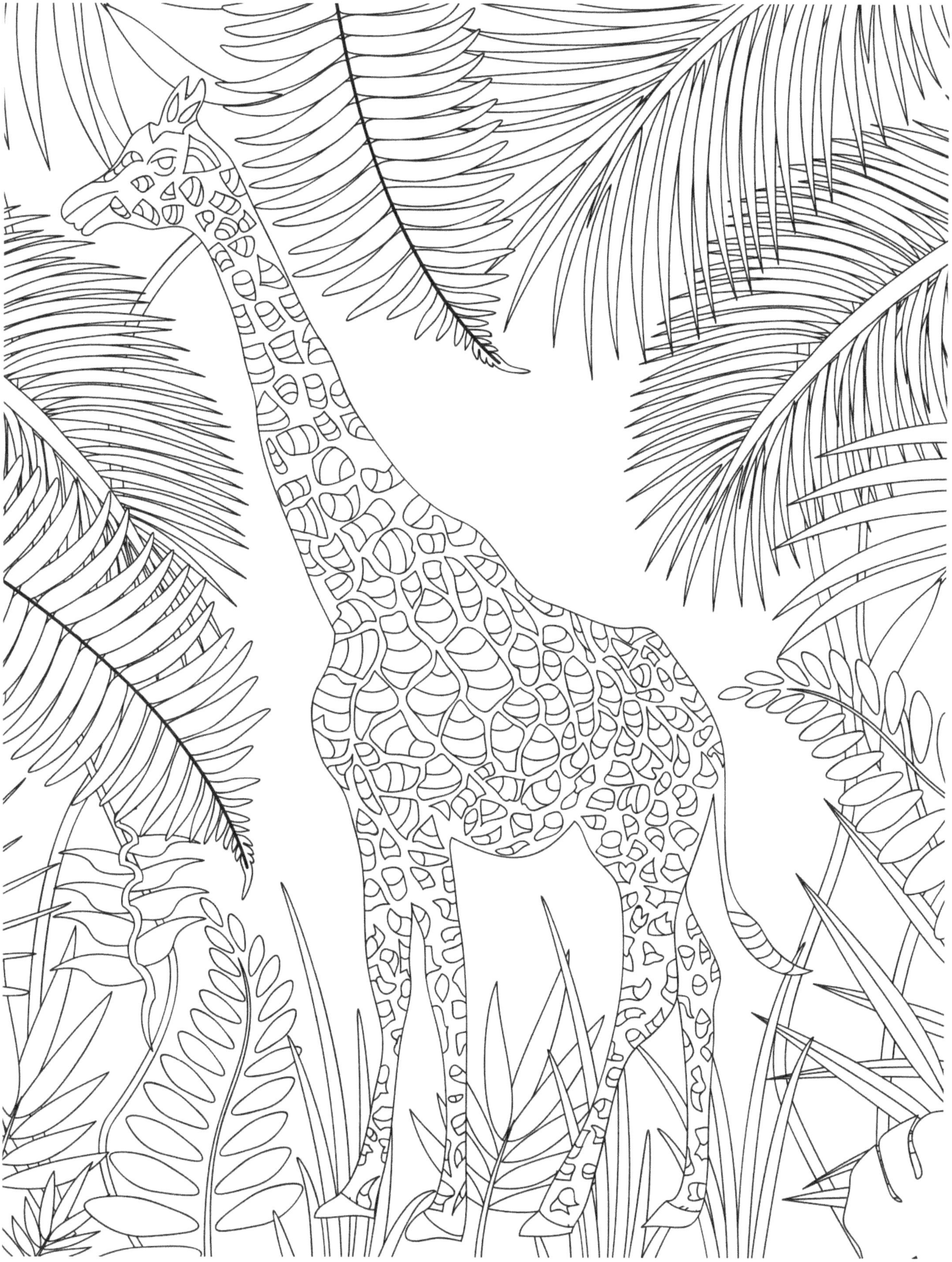

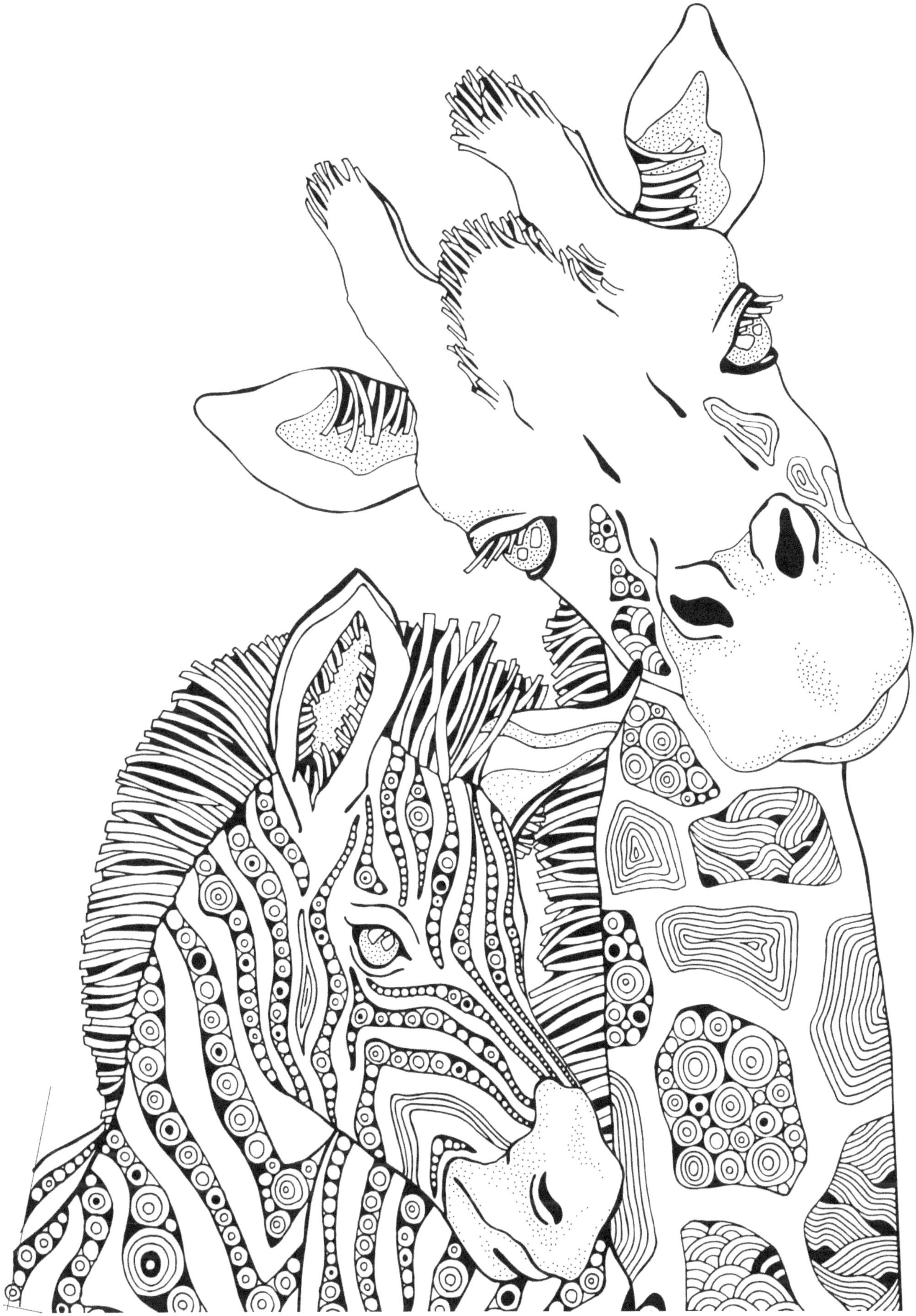

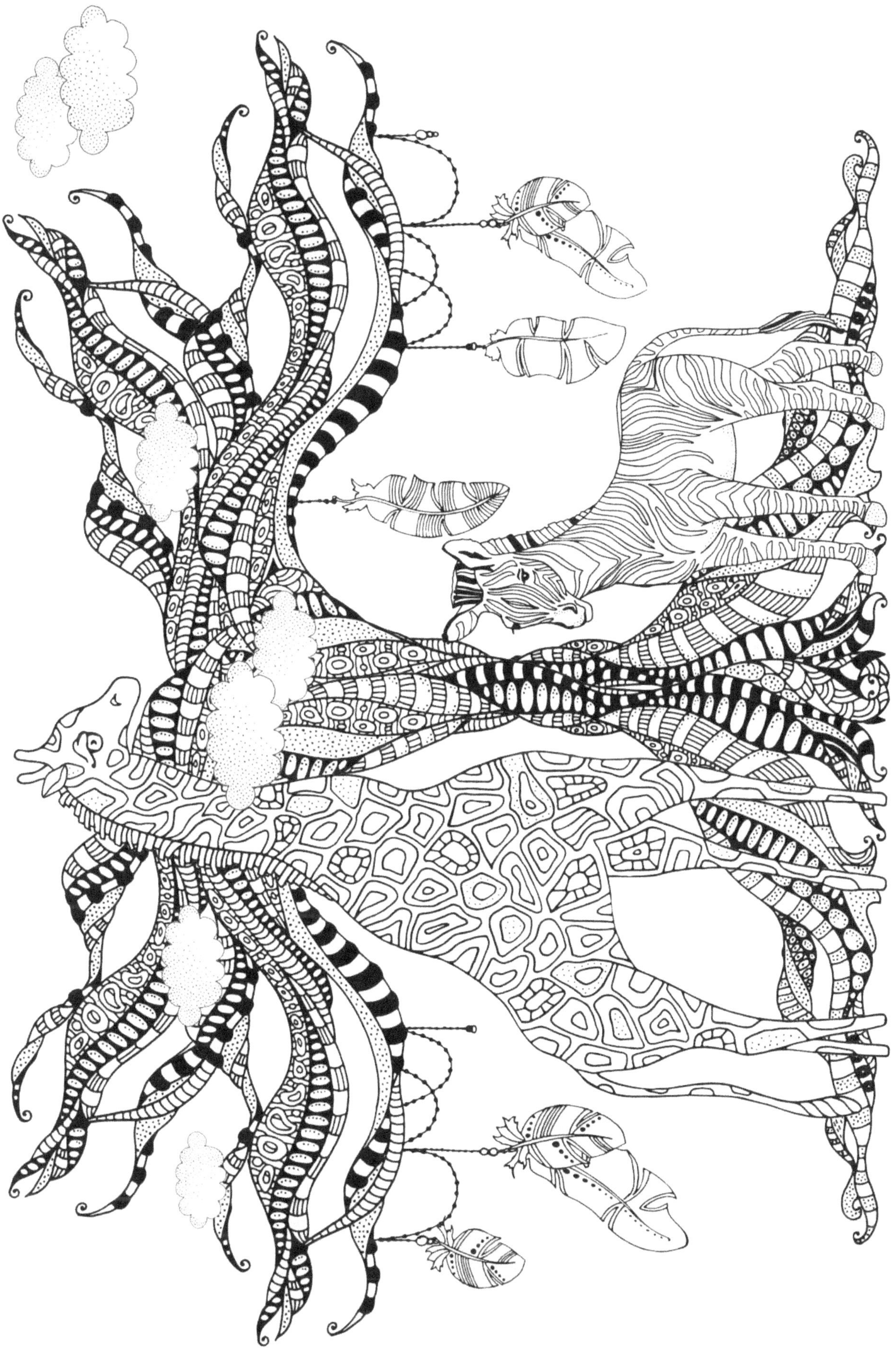

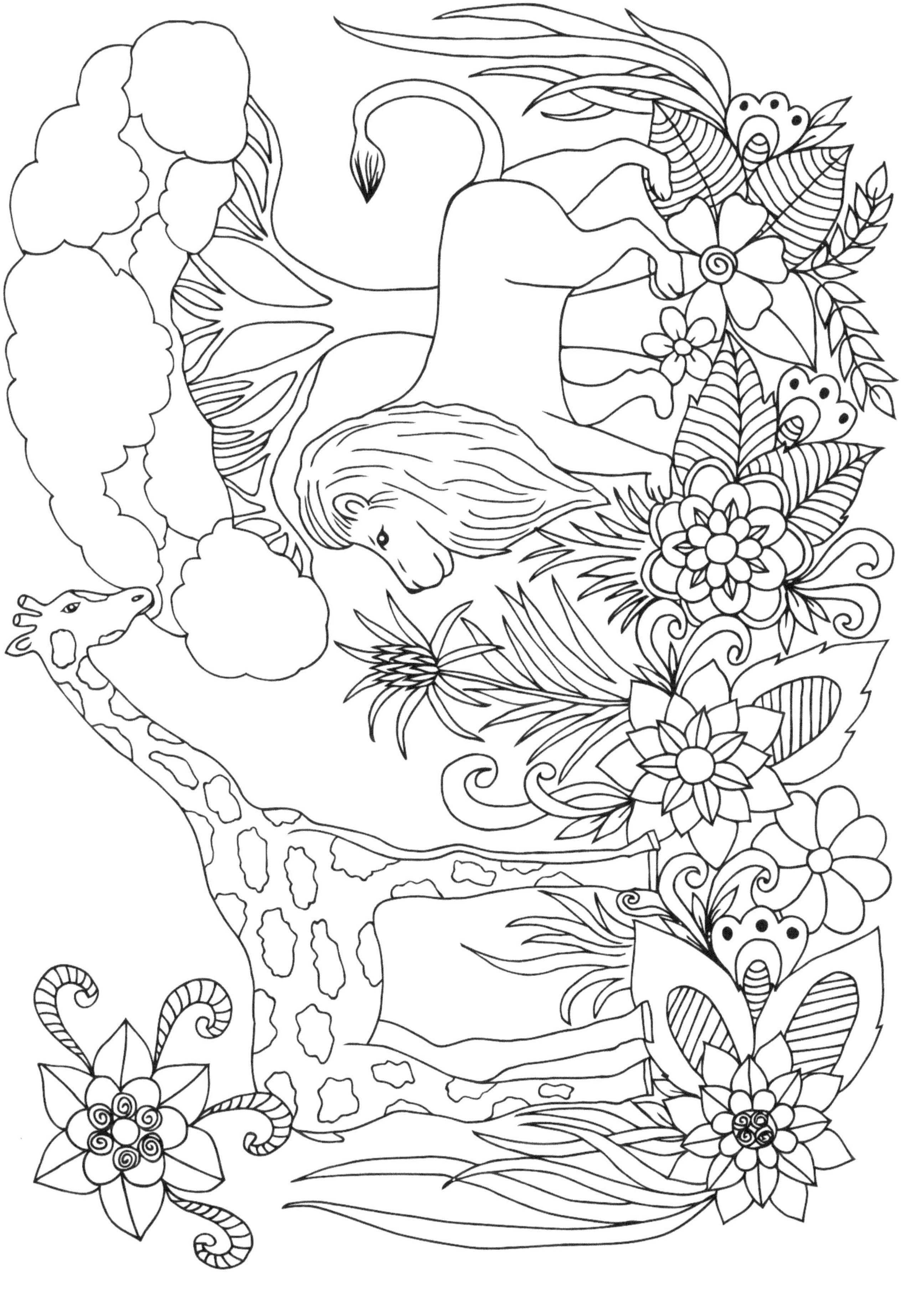

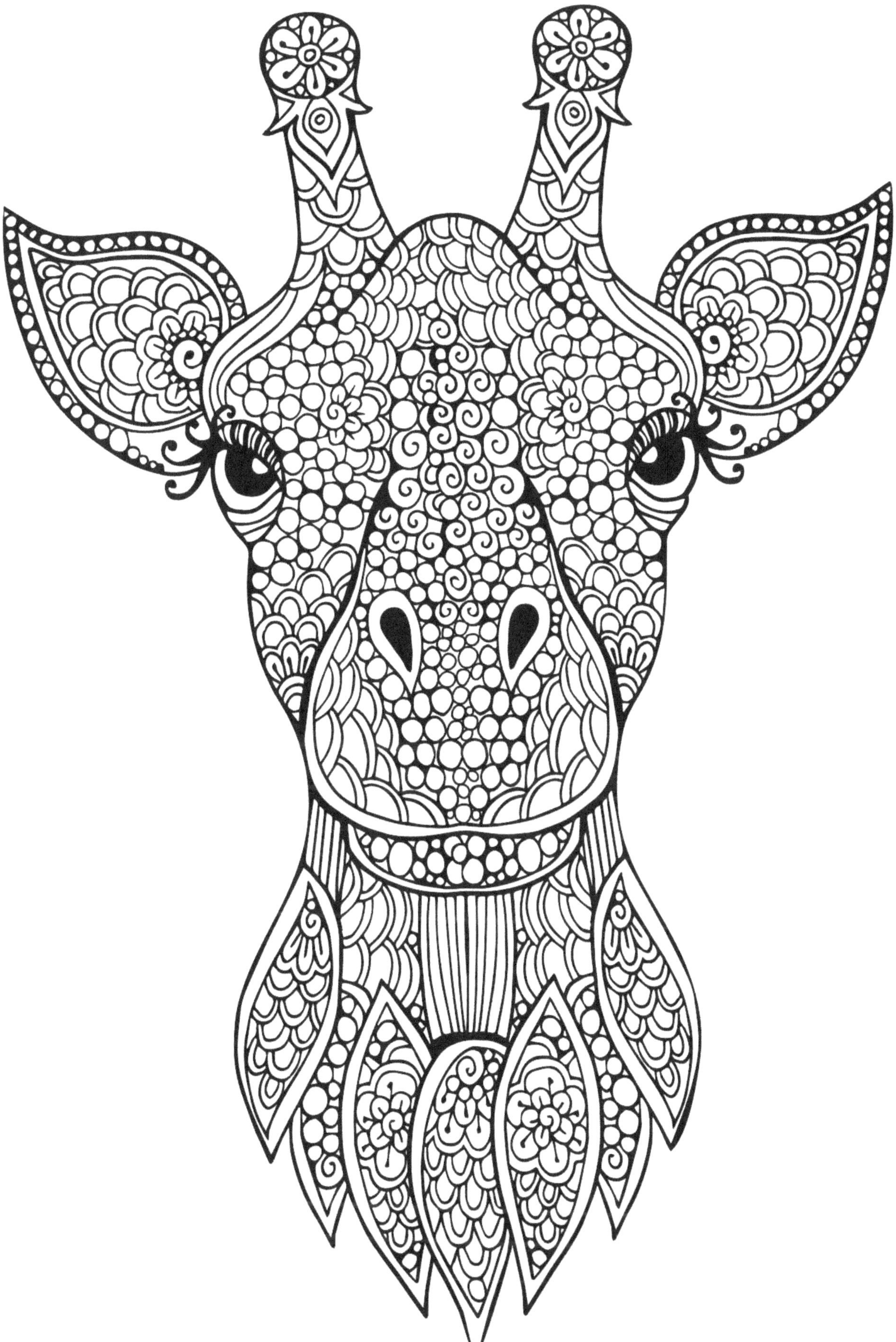

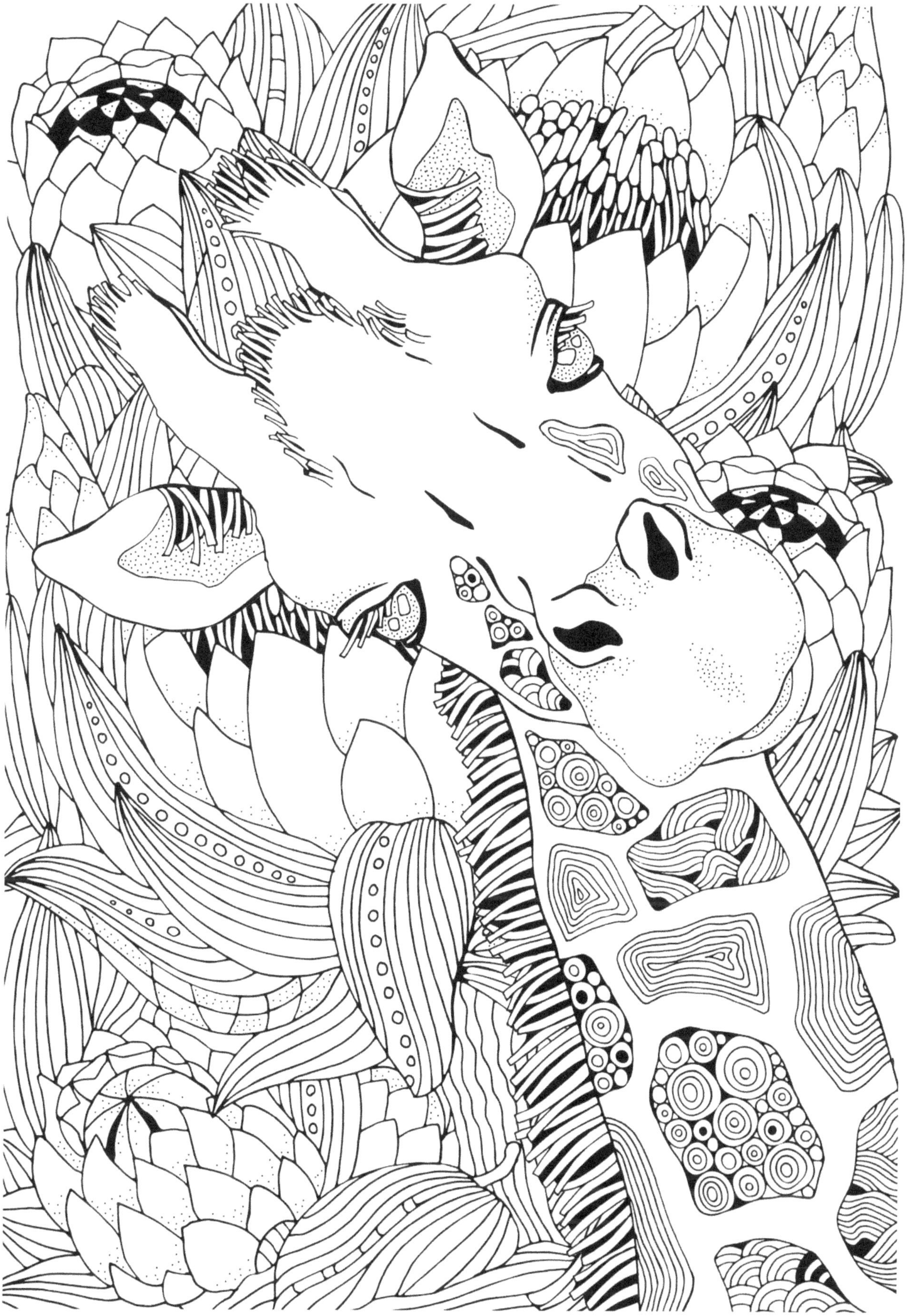

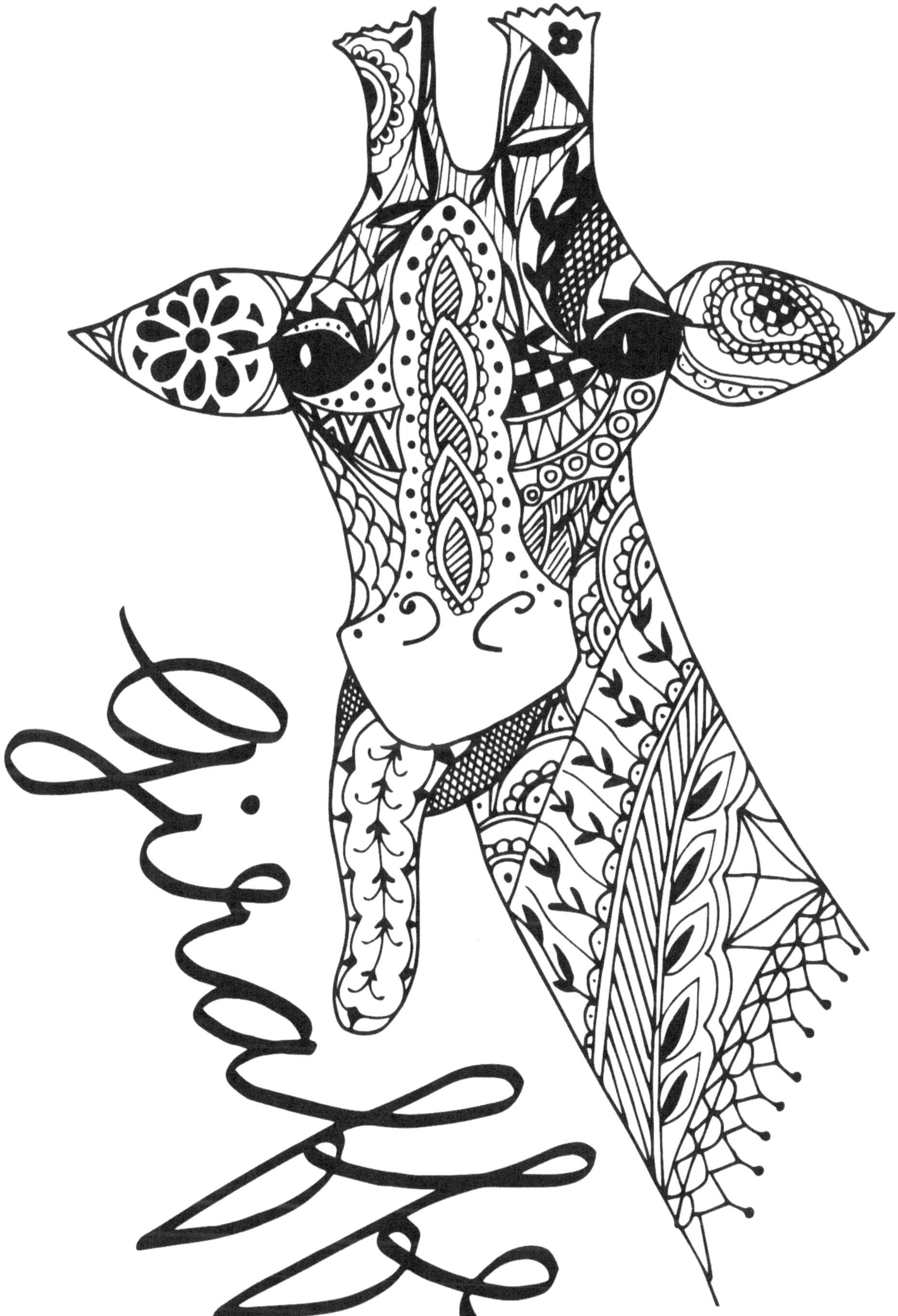
giraffe

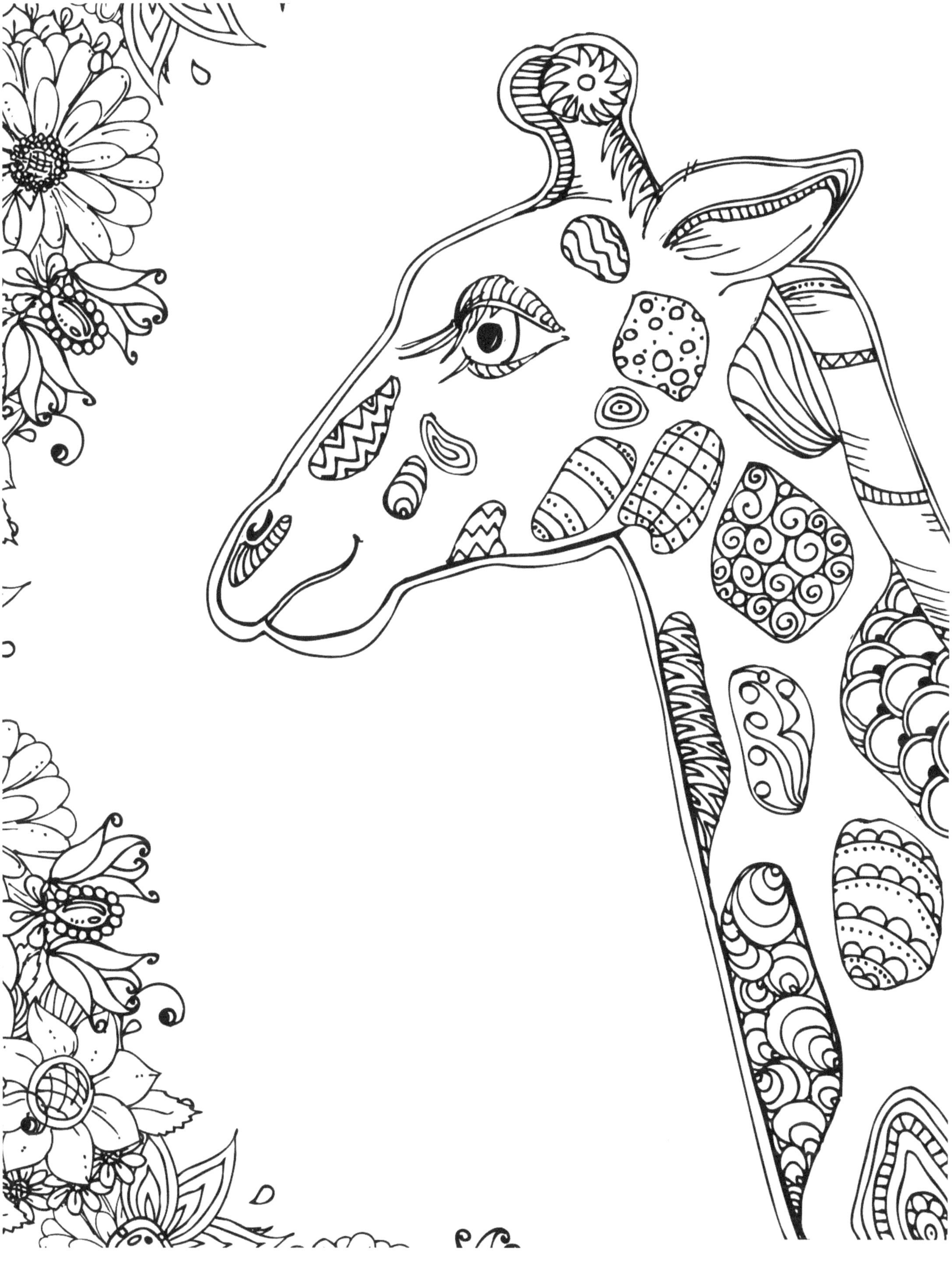

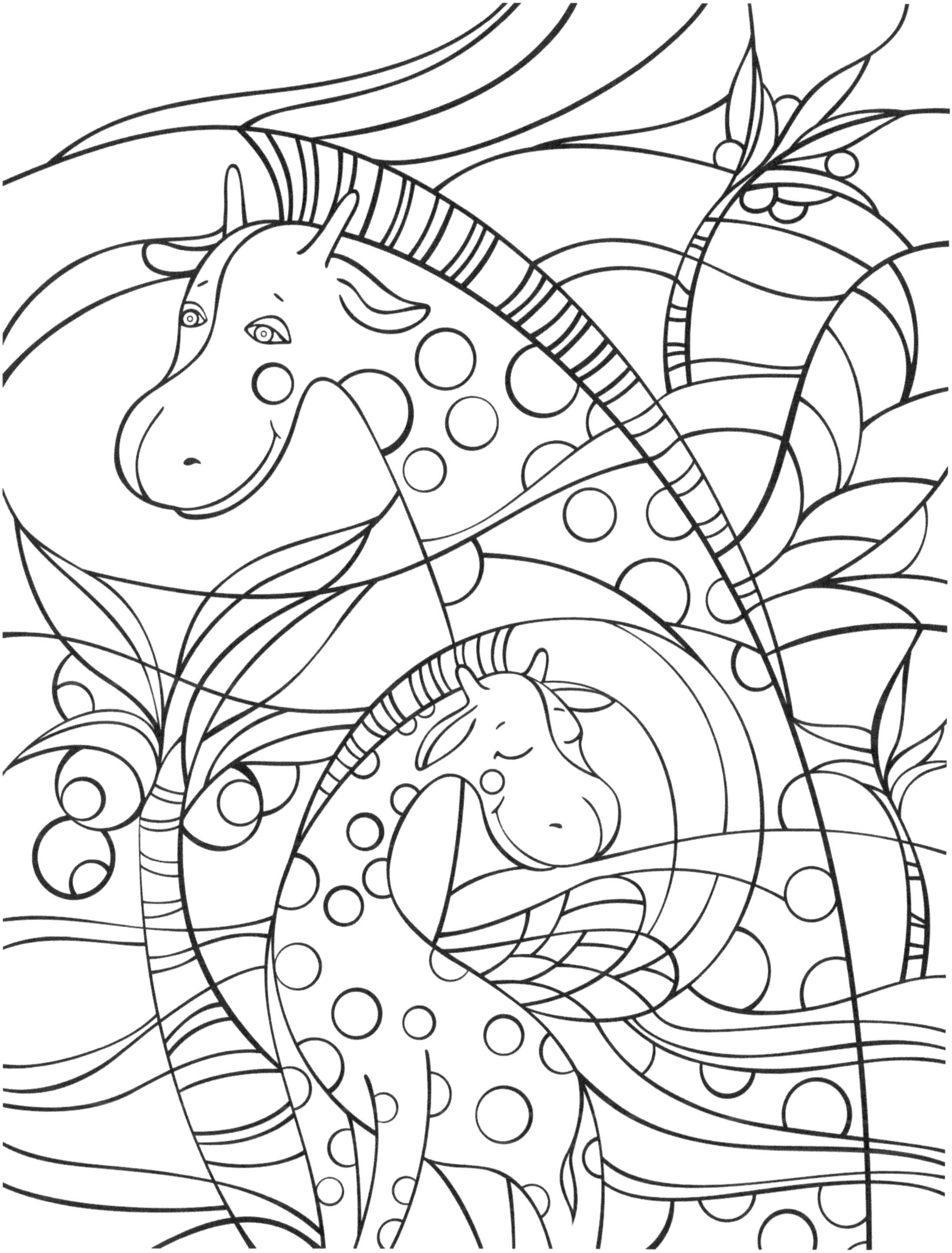

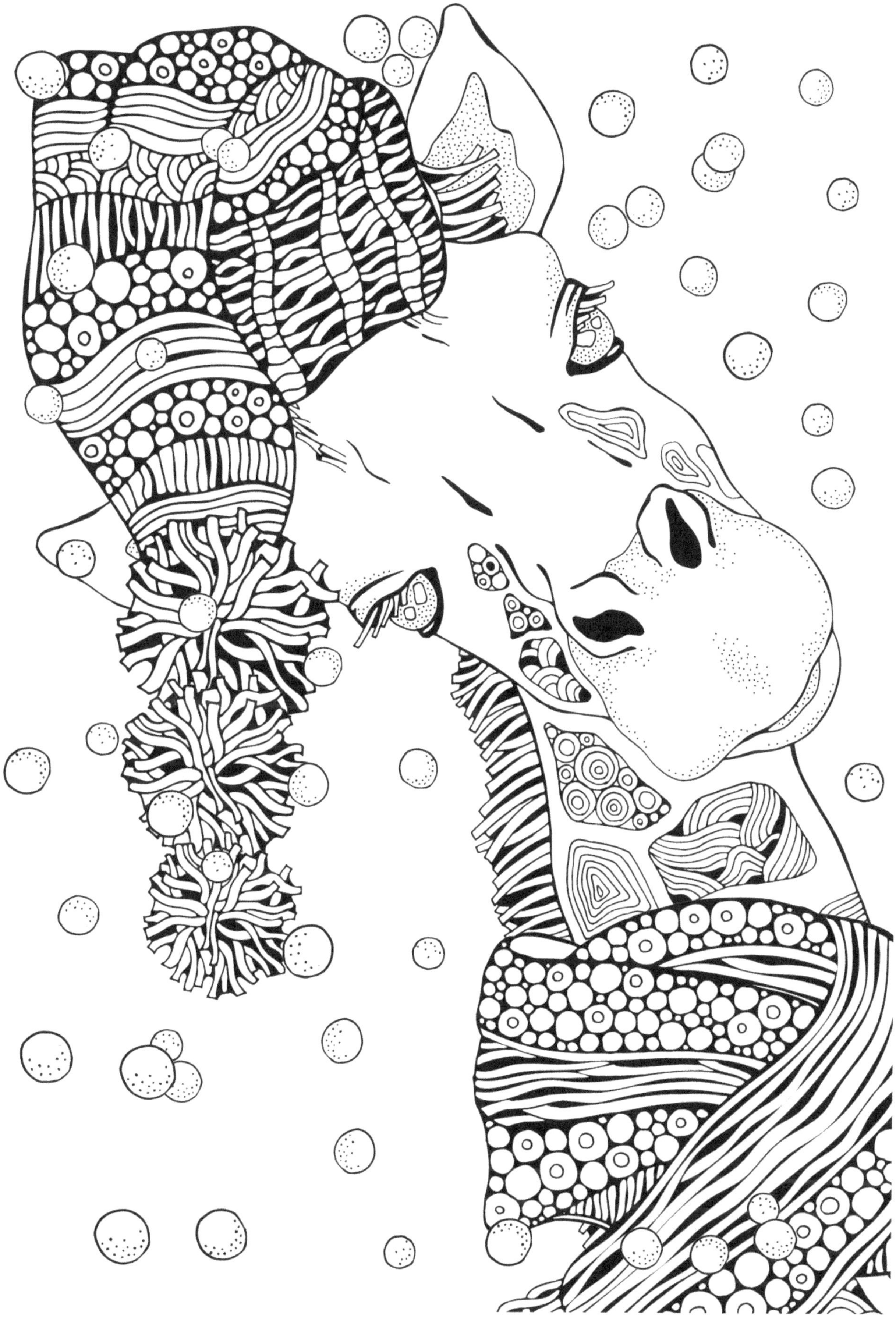

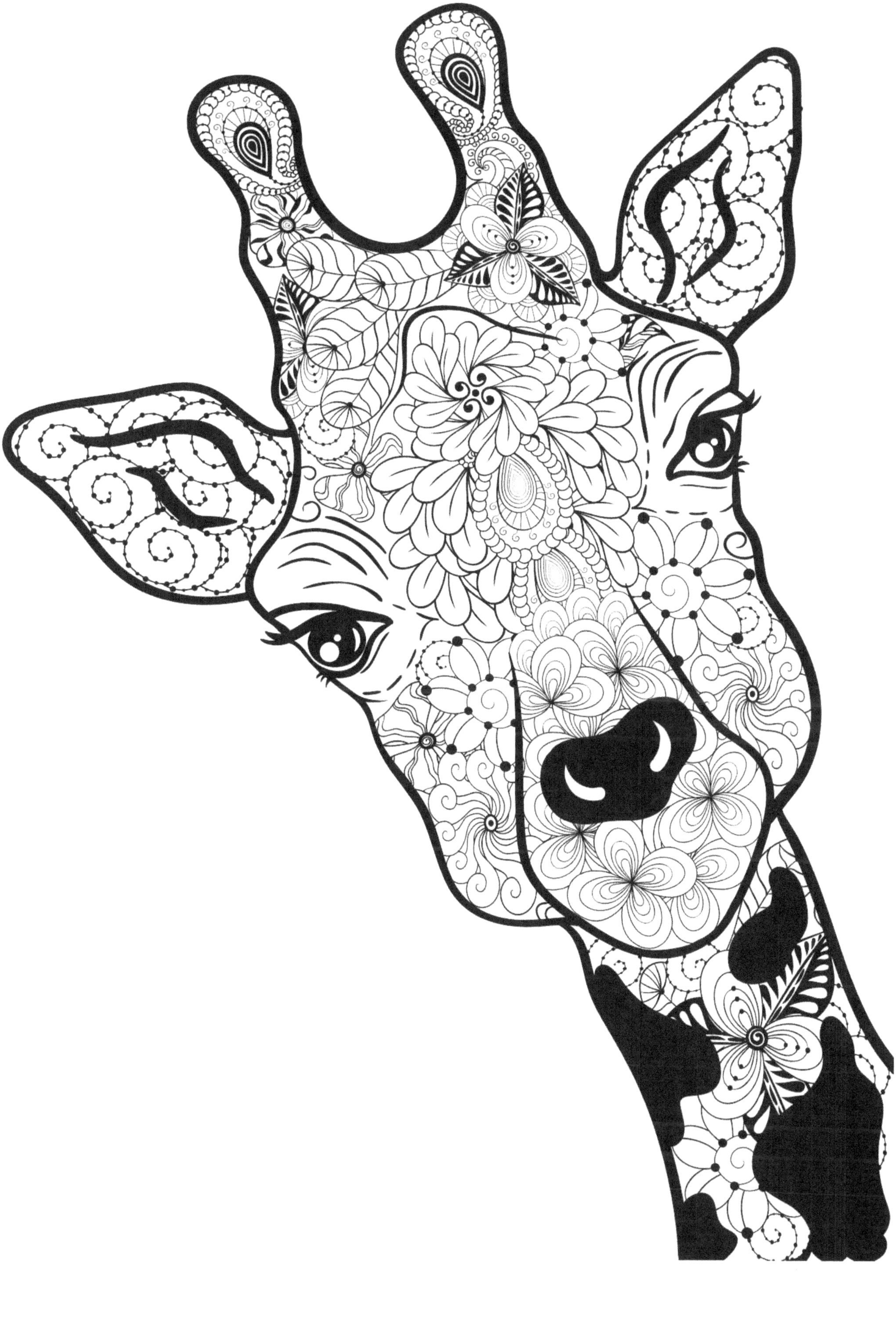

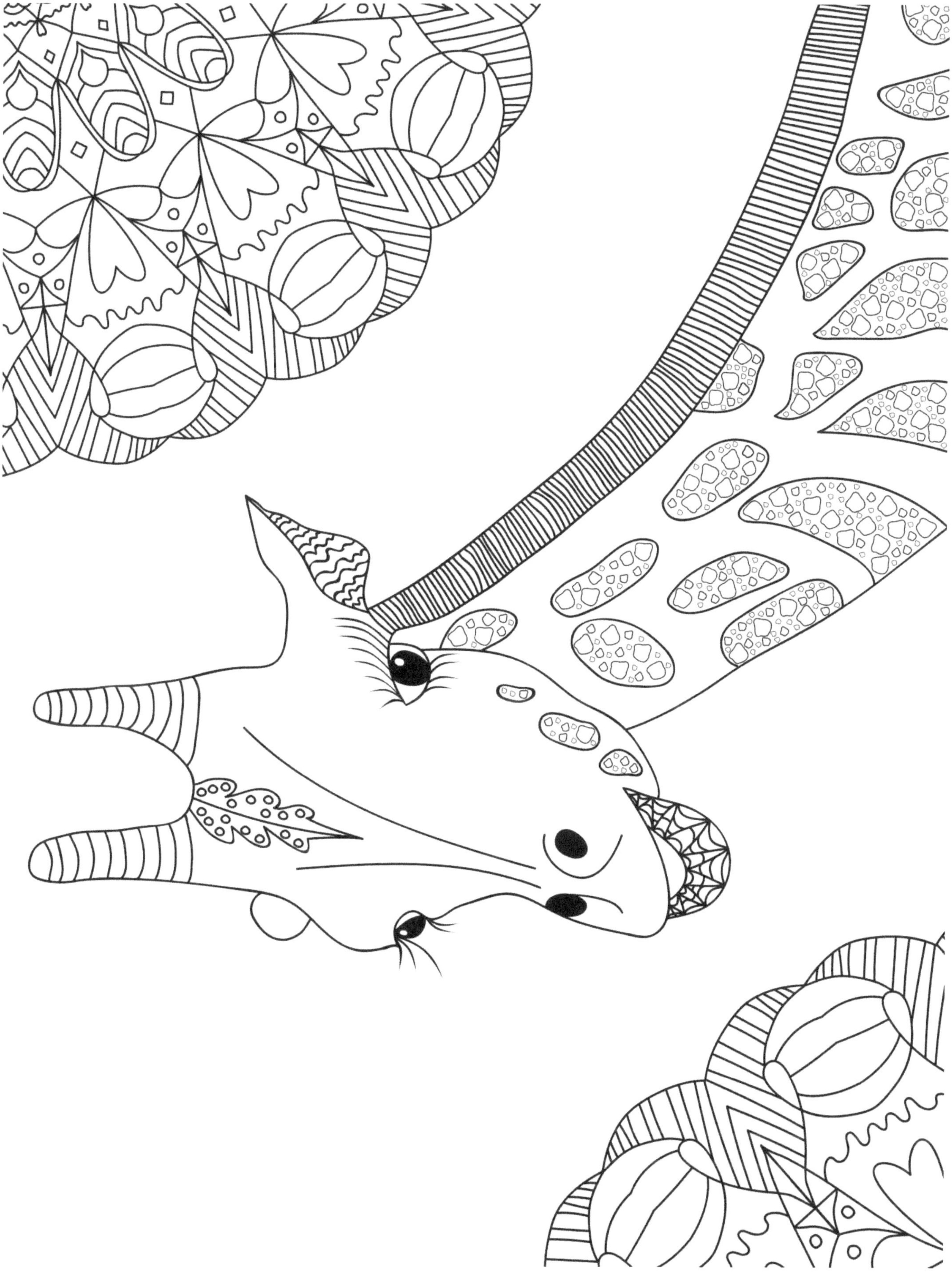

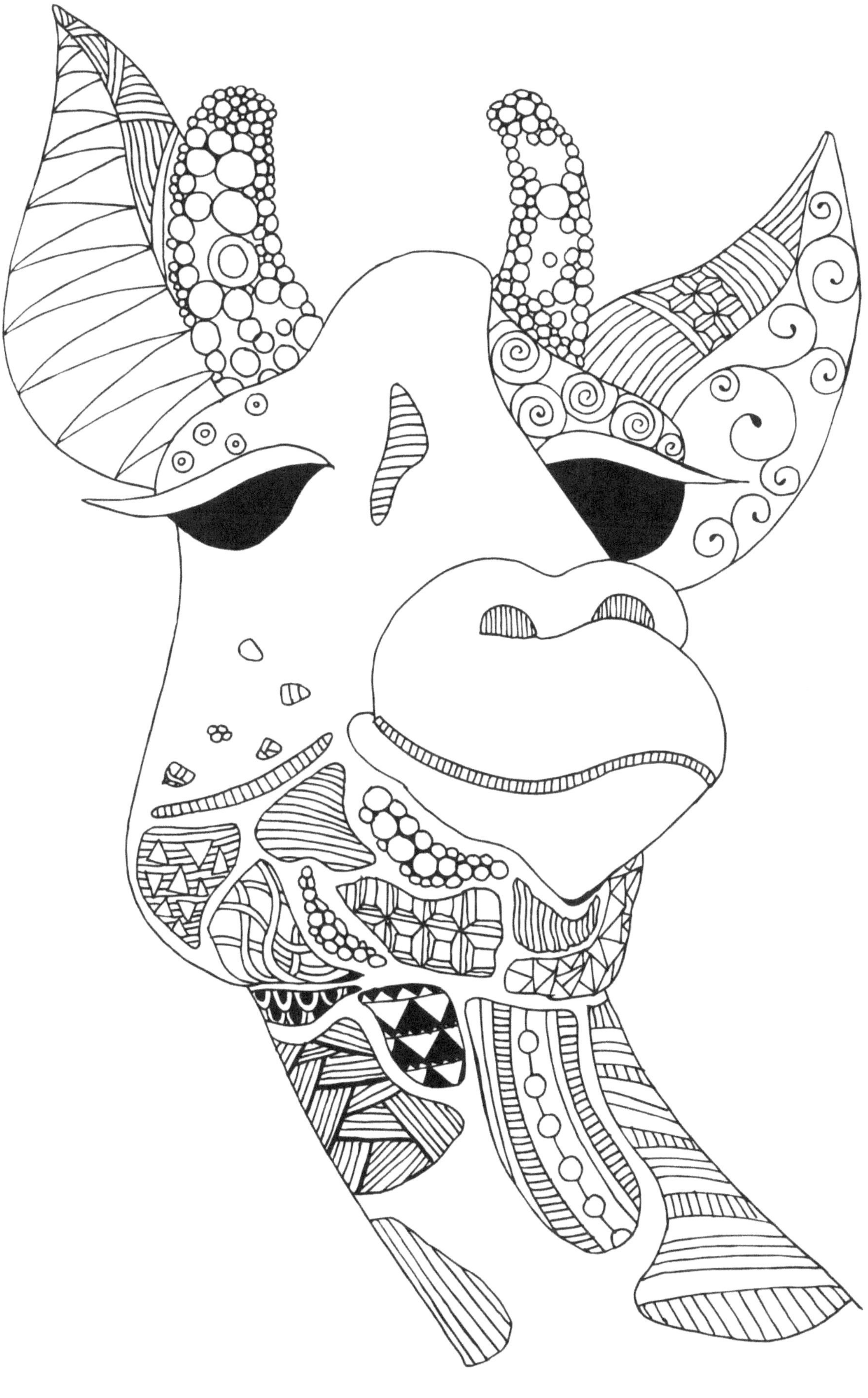

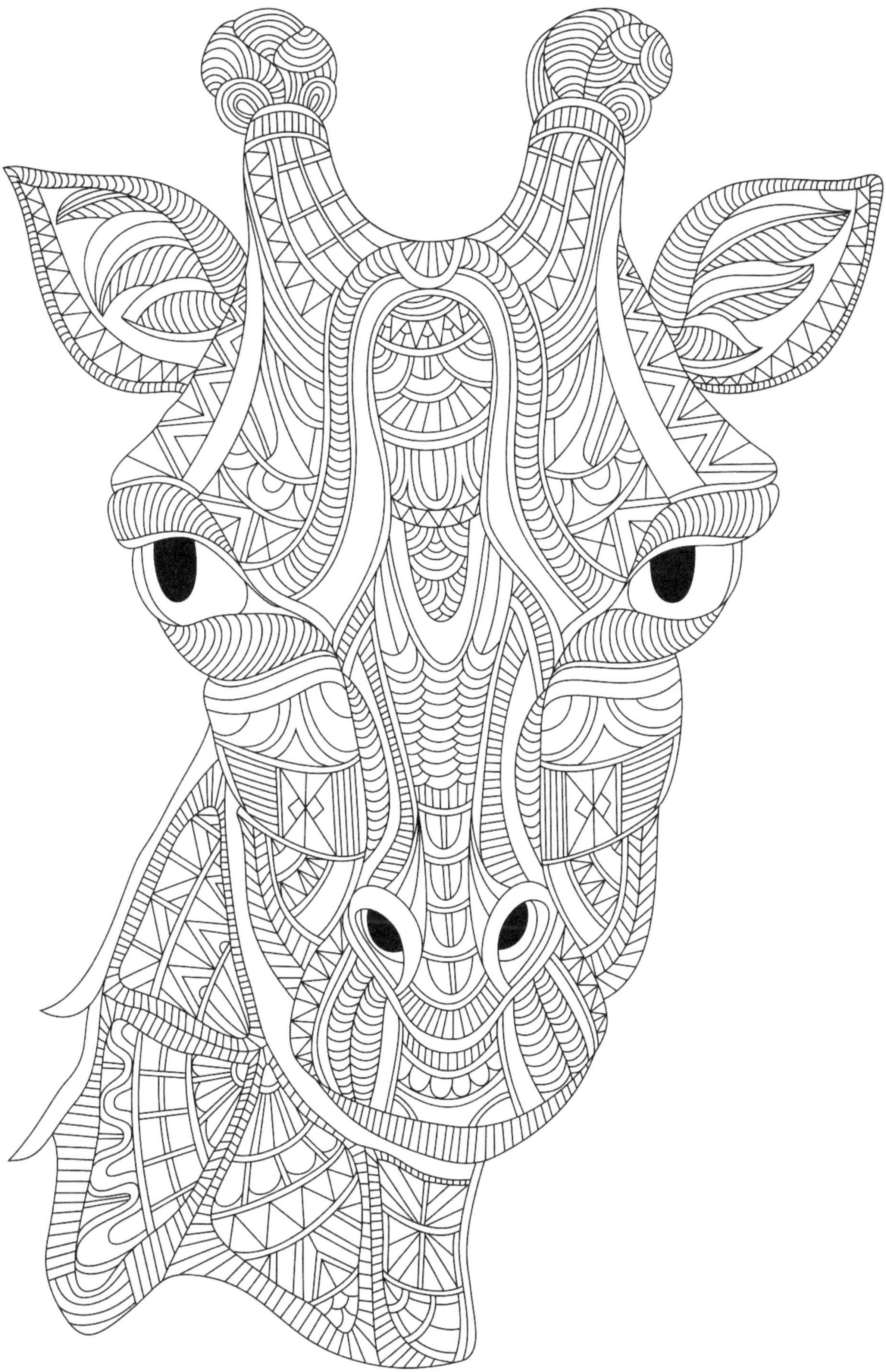

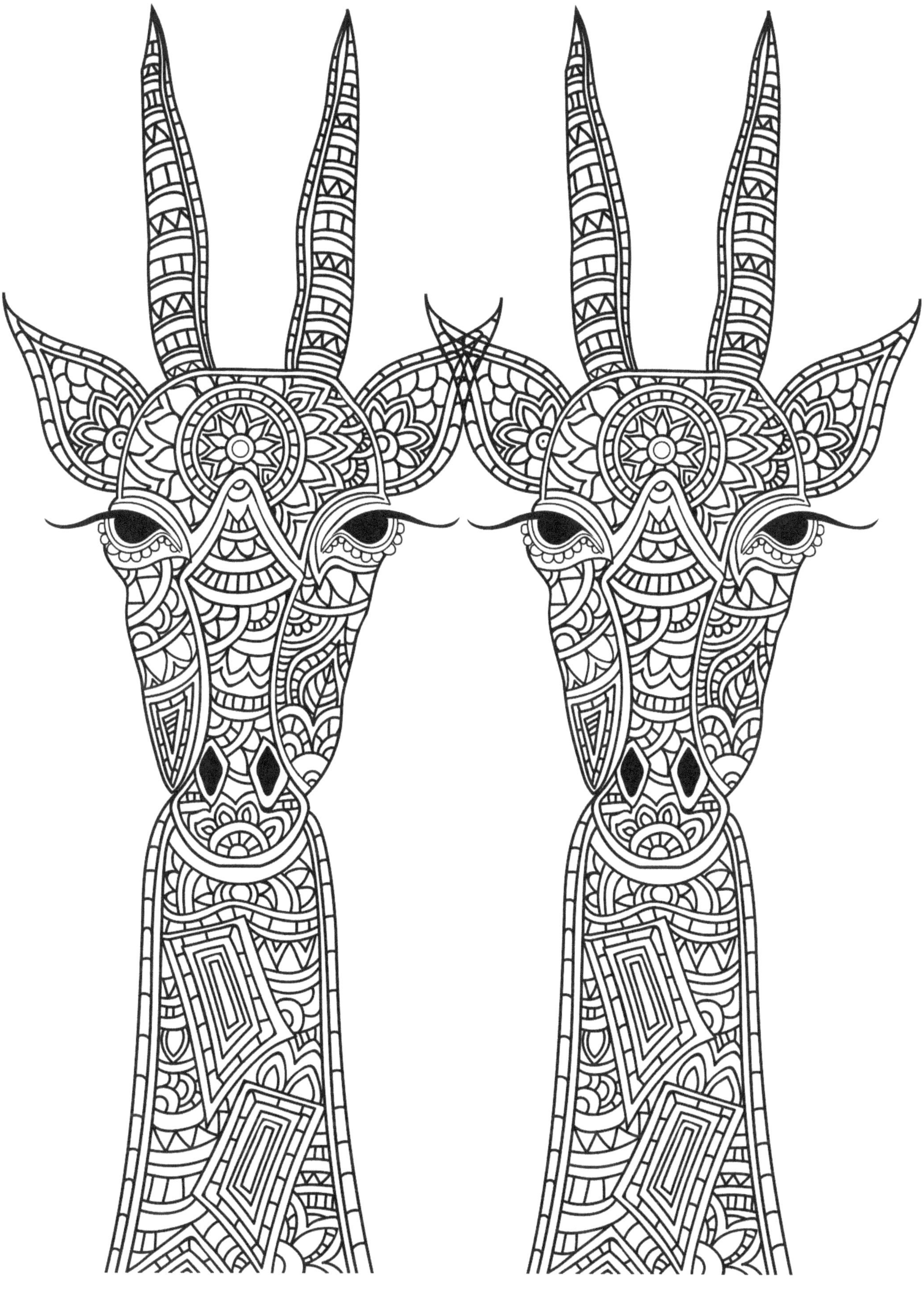

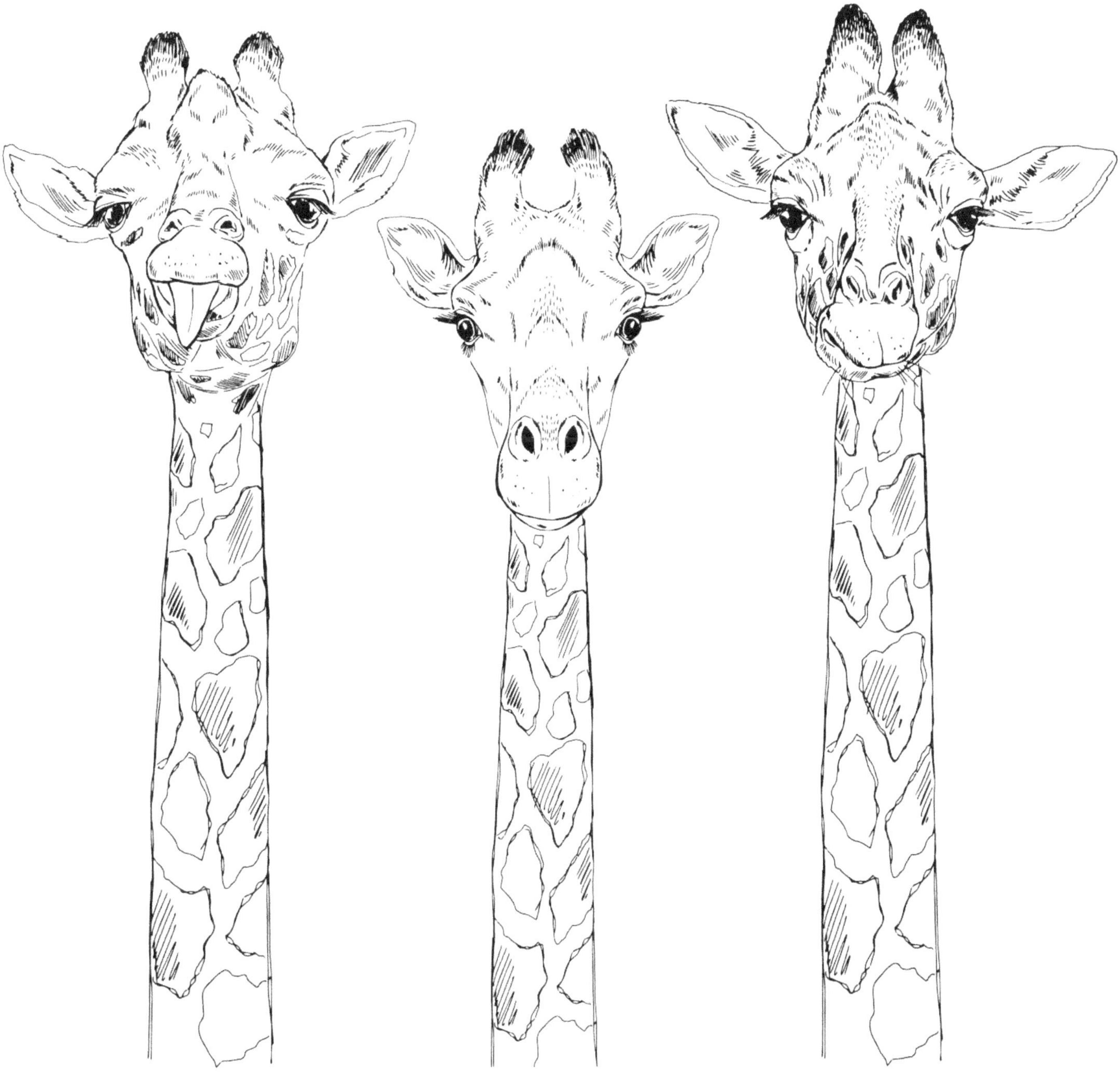

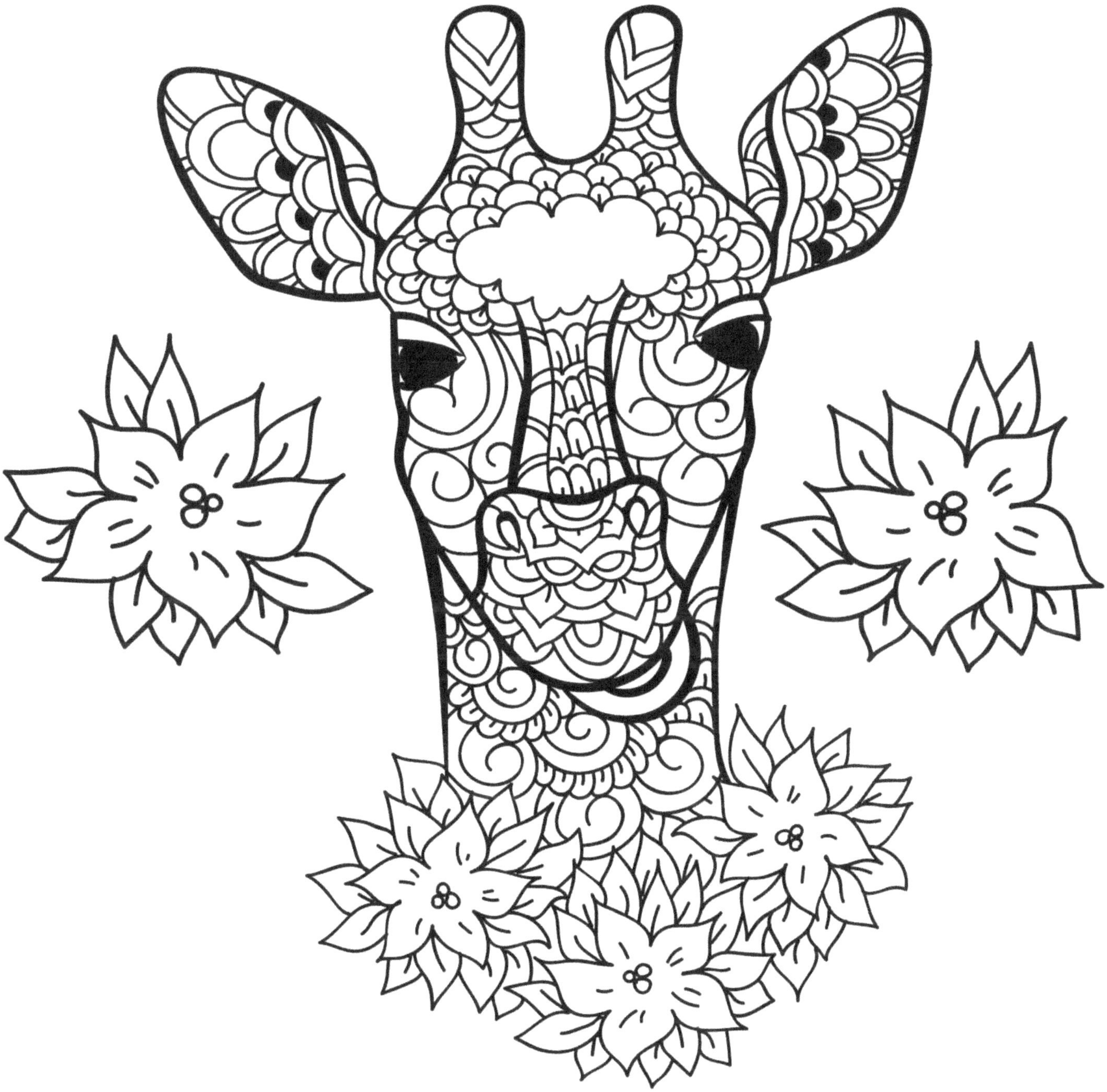

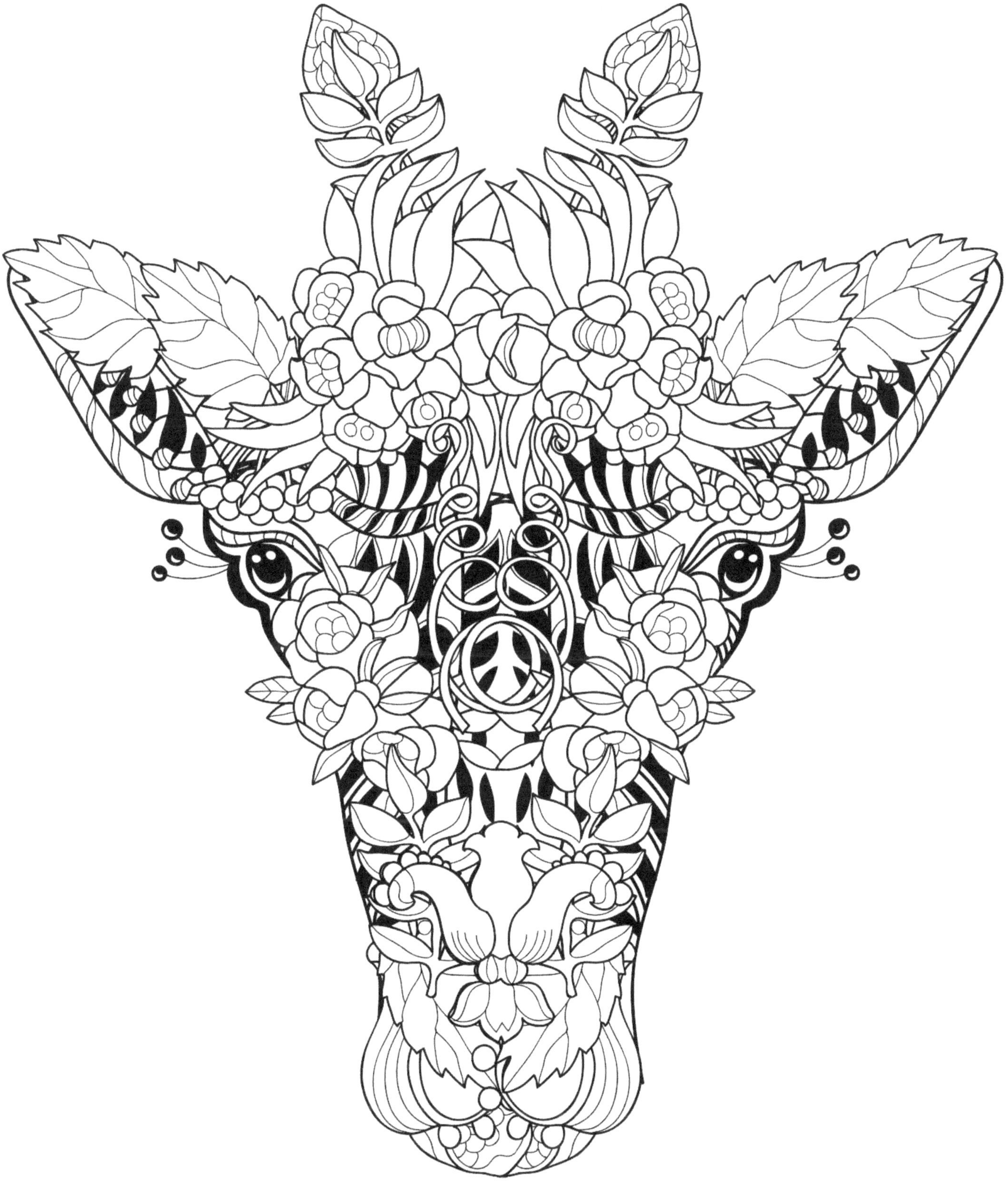

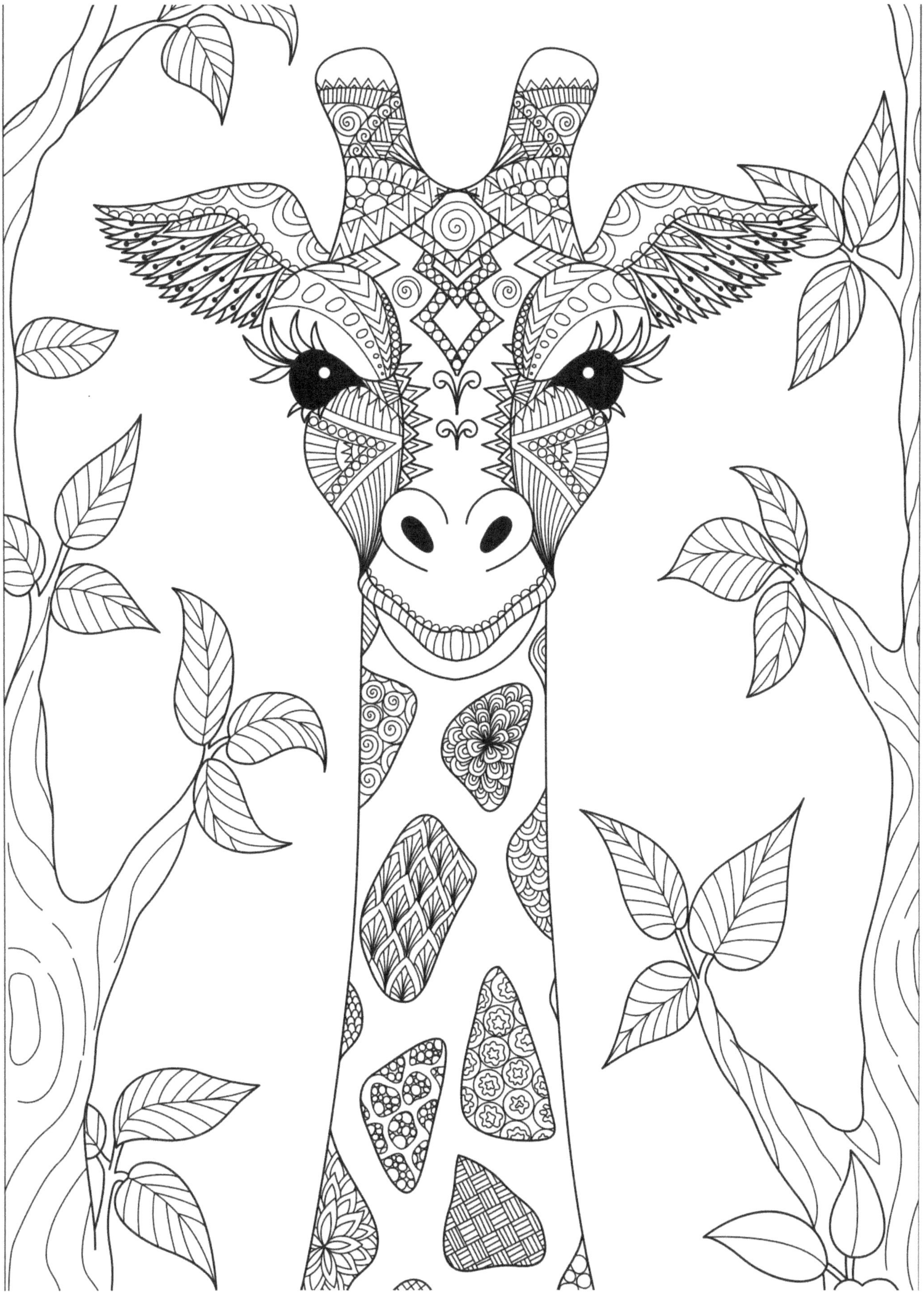

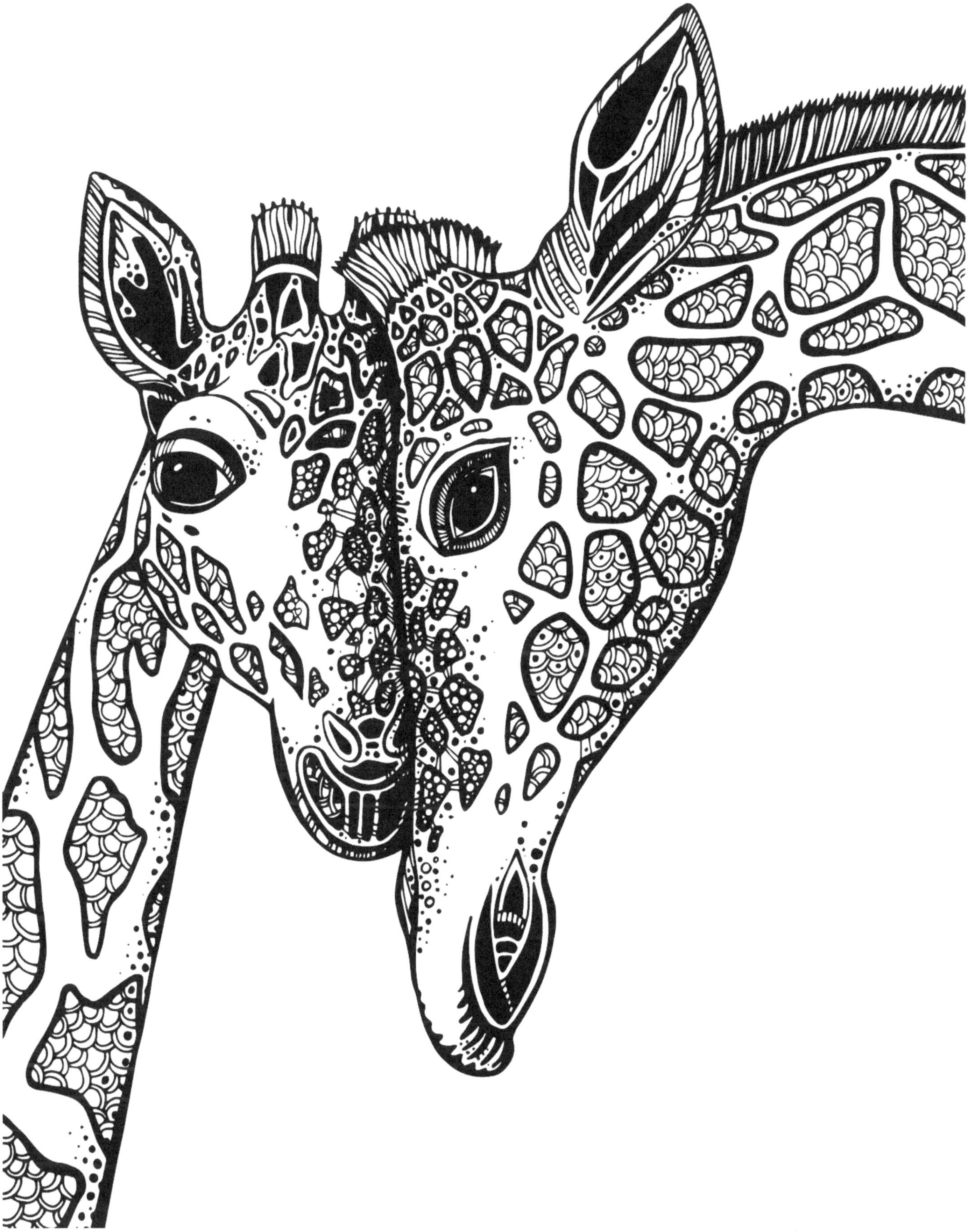

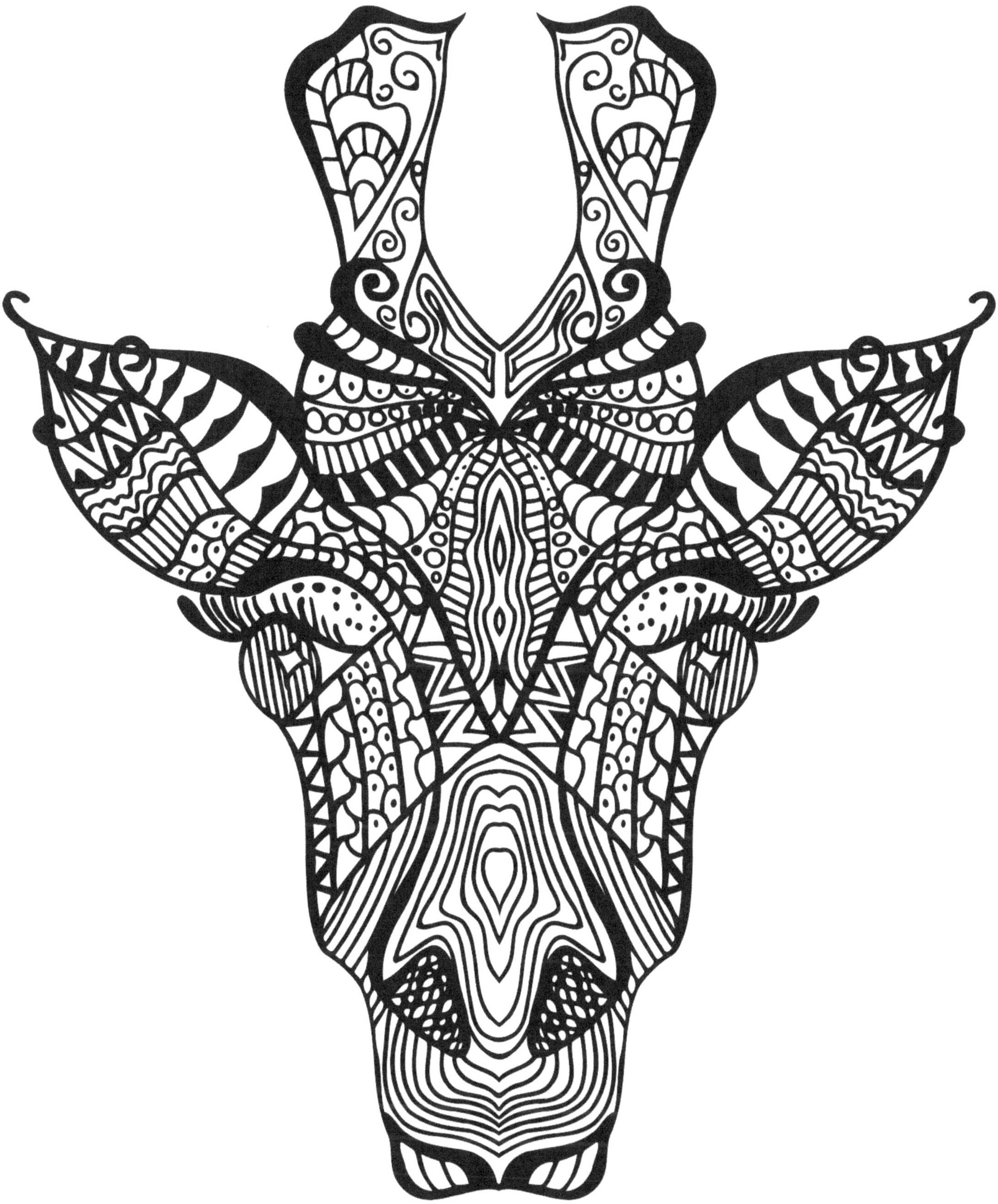

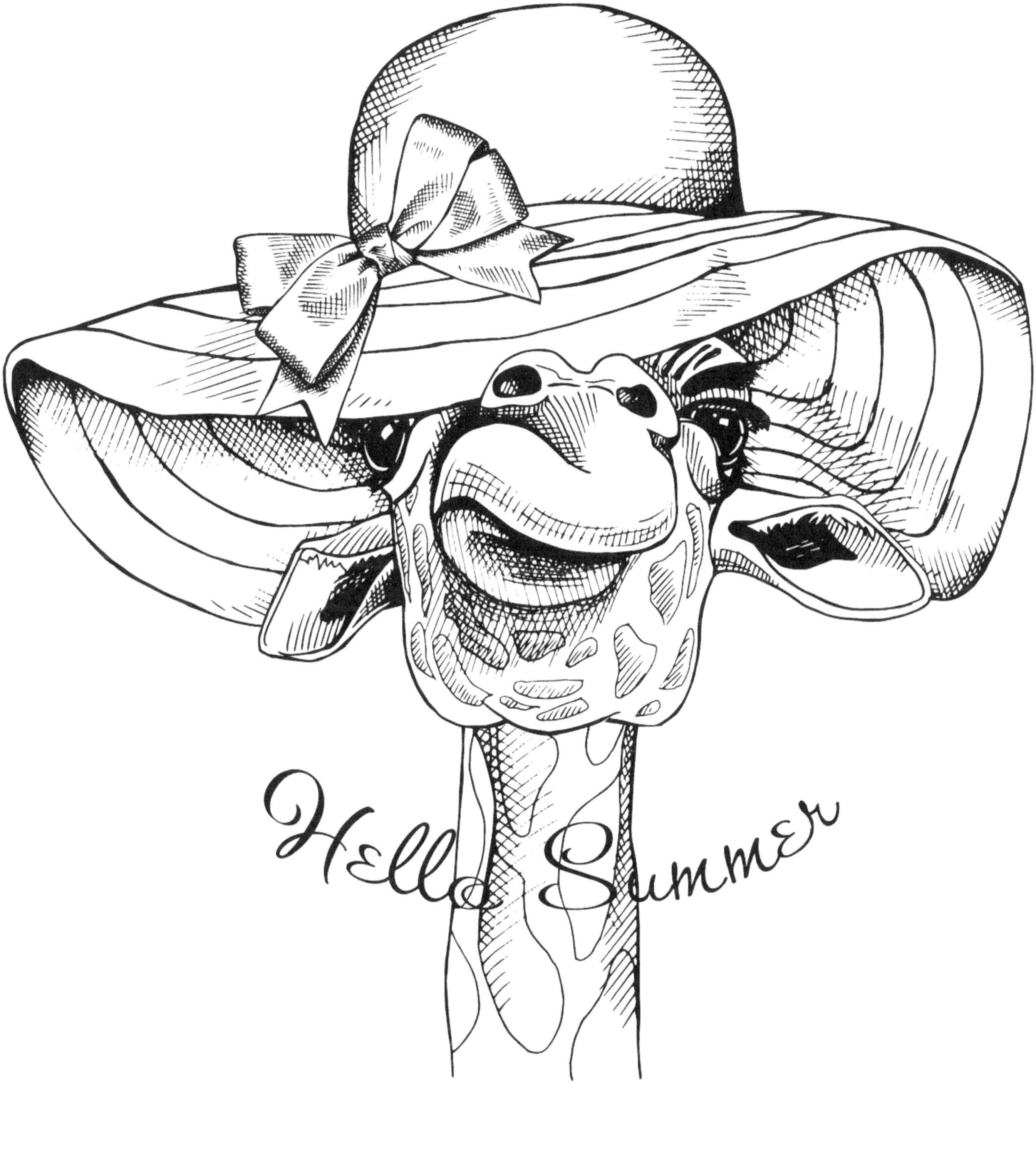
Hello Summer

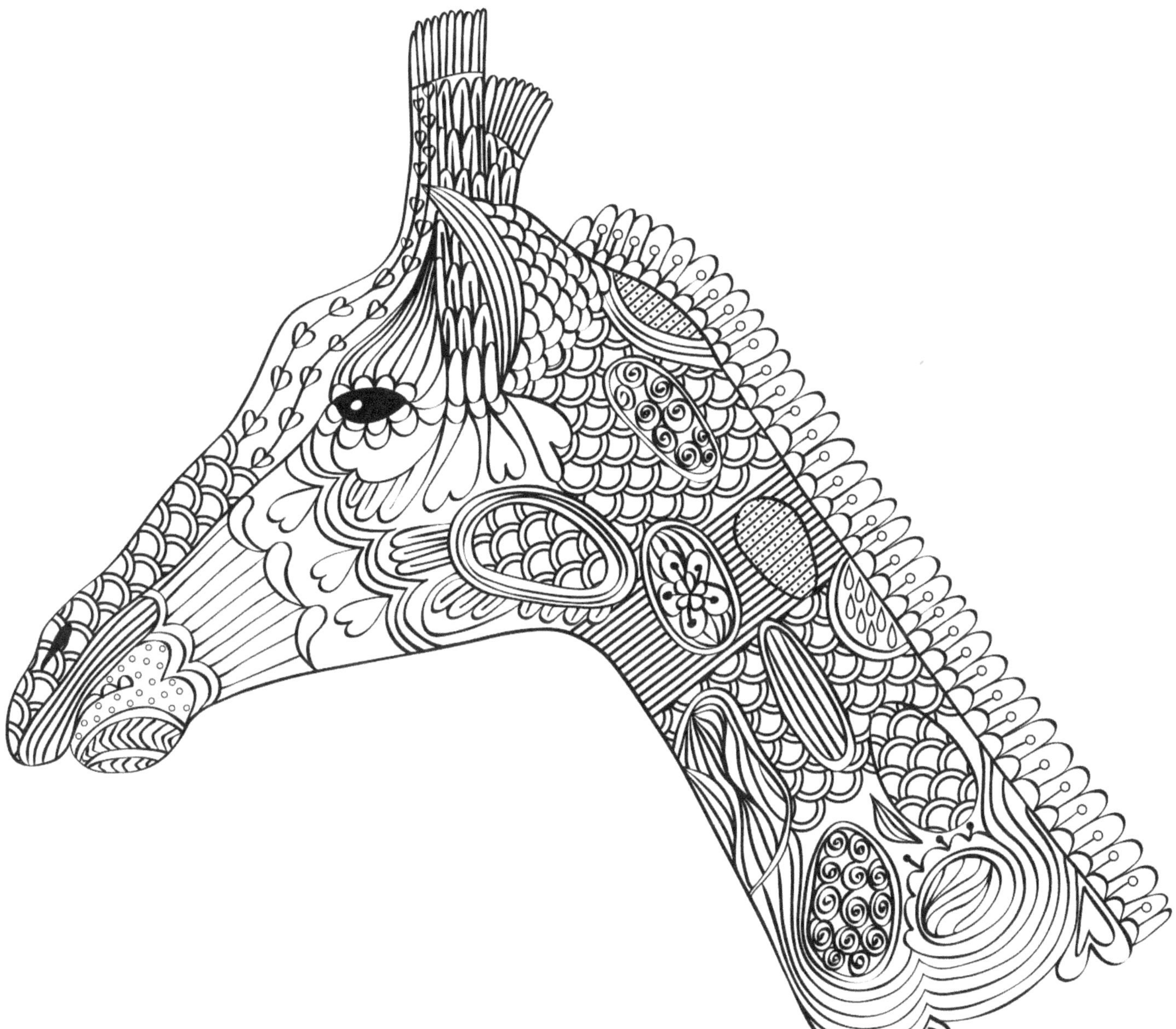

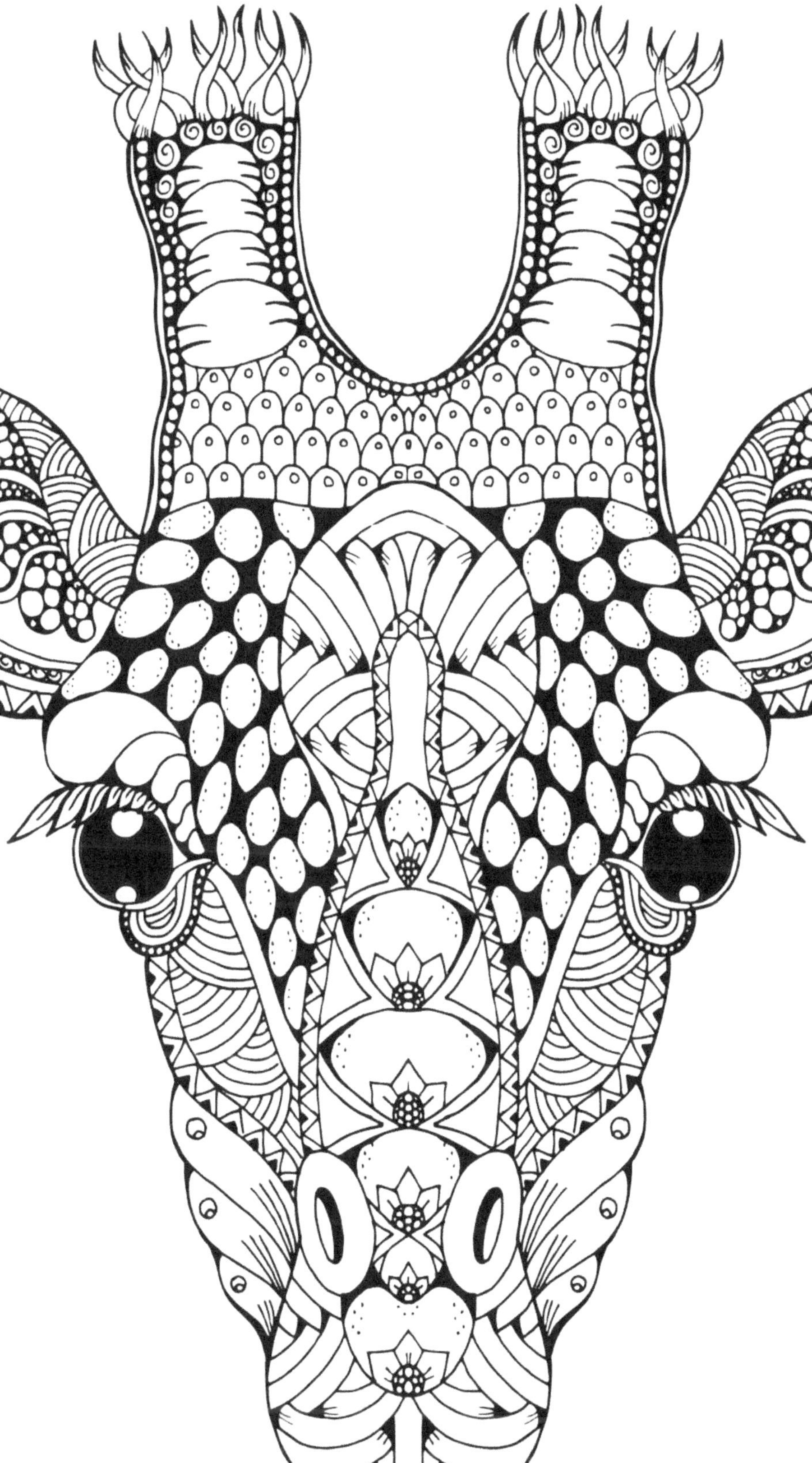

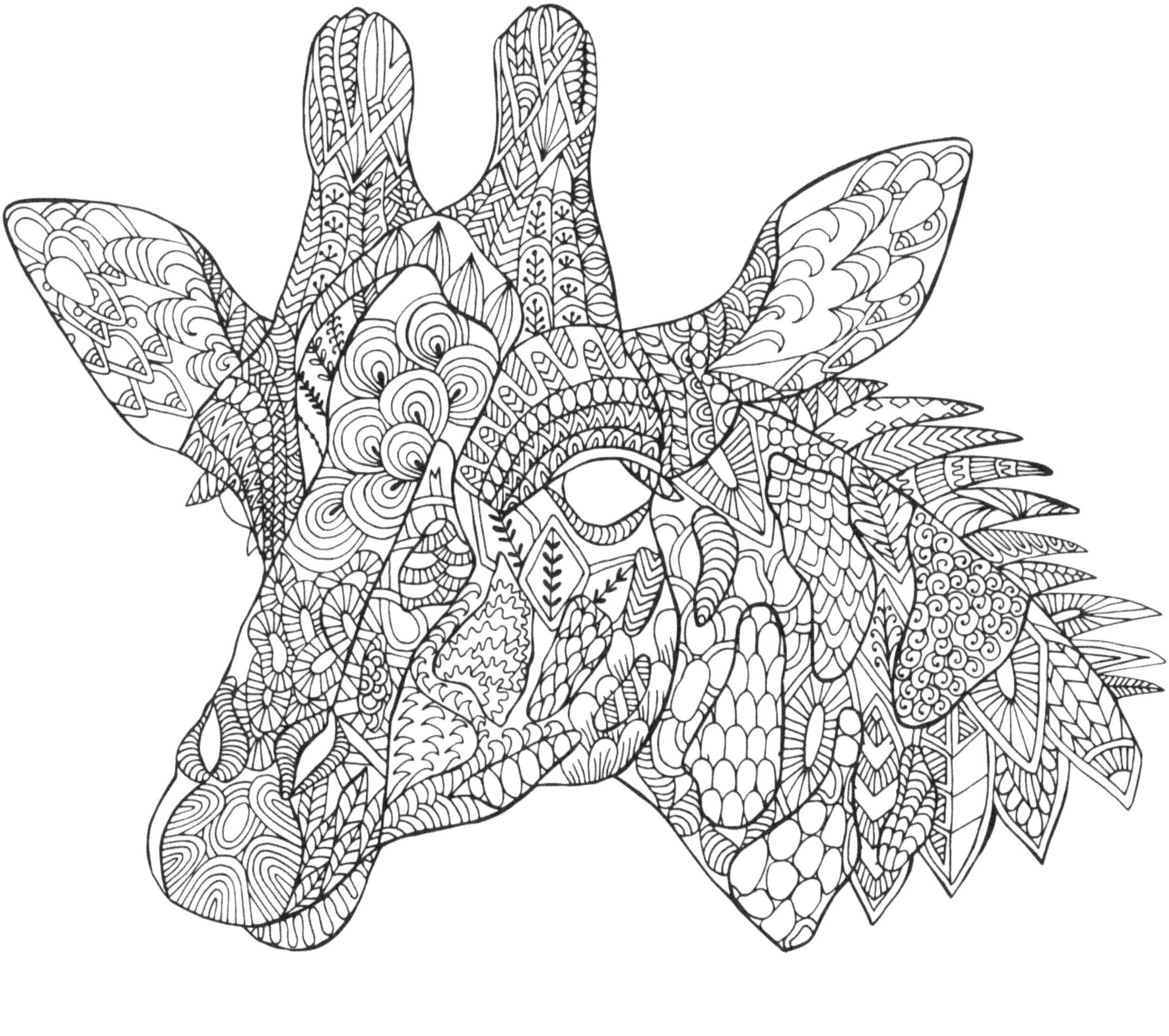

www.ingramcontent.com/pod-product-compliance
Lightning Source LLC
Chambersburg PA
CBHW081300180526
45170CB00007B/2509
* 9 7 8 1 5 4 5 3 3 8 7 8 0 *